Contents

Any words appearing in bold, **like this**, are explained in the Glossary.

Oil and its properties

All the objects we use are made from materials. Oil is a material. There are different sorts of oil. In this book you can find out about oil called crude oil or petroleum. We get many different materials from crude oil. The most important ones are **fuels**, such as petrol, and **raw materials** for making **plastic**.

This is what a pool of crude oil looks like under a microscope. It is very thick, like treacle.

Many objects, such as this toy, are made from plastic. Plastic is made from oil.

Properties tell us what a material is like. Crude oil is a thick **liquid**. It is dark brown and smelly. It is also inflammable, which means it burns easily. The materials we get from oil have many different properties. For example, butane and **bitumen** come from crude oil. Butane is a **gas**. It is a very good fuel. Bitumen is a sticky black **solid** that we use for making roads.

Don't use it!

The different properties of materials make them useful for different jobs. These properties can also make them unsuitable for some jobs. For example, we hardly ever use crude oil as we find it. It is too smoky to burn and too thick to use as **lubricating** *oil.*

Where does oil come from?

Crude oil is a **natural** material. The crude oil we use today was formed over millions of years from the remains of dead animals and plants that lived in the sea. When the animals and plants died, their remains sank to the bottom of the sea. They were gradually buried in layers of rock. Over millions of years the remains turned into oil. Because oil is made from dead plants and animals we call it a **fossil fuel**.

Oil wells can be drilled from oil rigs in the middle of the sea.

This huge pipeline carries crude oil from oil wells to oil **refineries**. Crude oil is also moved by oil tankers on land and sea.

Finding oil

Crude oil is trapped in rocks deep underground or deep under the sea. Scientists called **geologists**, who study rocks, try to work out where oil might be. They drill into the rocks to see if they contain oil. The holes they drill are called oil wells. If there is oil, long pipes are put down the well and the oil flows up to the surface. Many people work at searching for oil and getting it out of the ground.

Oil refining

Crude oil is made up of many different substances mixed together. Some of the substances are **gases**, some are thin **liquids**, some are thick liquids and some are **solids**. The substances are called hydrocarbons because they are mainly made up of carbon and hydrogen.

This is the part of an oil refinery where the crude oil is heated to make it split up.

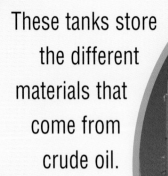

These tanks store the different materials that come from crude oil.

We split crude oil up into its different parts. This process is called **refining** and it happens at an oil refinery. The crude oil is slowly heated up until it becomes mostly gases. These gases cool down in a special machine. Each gas turns into a liquid at a different temperature – so each one can be collected separately.

Oil in history

*Thousands of years ago people used oil, which they found seeping from the ground, as a **fuel** in oil lamps. Boat builders used thick **bitumen** from dried oil to make their boats **waterproof**. People did not begin to drill for oil until about 150 years ago.*

Oil for fuel

Petrol is one of the most important materials we get from crude oil. It is also called gasoline. Petrol is a colourless **liquid**. It gives off smelly **gases** called **fumes**. Petrol burns very well. It makes lots of heat that we can use.

At a petrol station fuel is stored in underground tanks.

Most petrol is called unleaded because it does not contain a substance called lead. Lead used to be added to petrol to make engines work better.

Most petrol is used as a **fuel** for cars and motorbikes. They have an engine called a petrol engine. Inside the engine the petrol is made into tiny drops and mixed with air. The mixture goes into the engine's cylinders and burns, making small explosions. This makes the engine's **pistons** move. In turn, the pistons make the wheels move.

Don't use it!
Petrol fumes are very explosive. We cannot use petrol as a fuel for things like barbecues or oil lamps. The fumes would explode. We must use fuels that burn slowly, such as charcoal or vegetable oil.

Trucks, ships and planes

Kerosene, diesel oil and **fuel** oil are more fuels that we get from crude oil. They are all colourless **liquids**. We use them to make engines work, to make heat, for heating and cooking, and for lighting.

Most kerosene is used as a fuel for aircraft jet engines. Kerosene burns very well, giving jet engines their huge power. It is also burned in kerosene heaters. In many parts of the world it is also used as a fuel in lamps.

The kerosene used in jet engines must be very clean or the engines could be damaged.

Most big trucks have an engine that burns diesel oil.

Diesel oil is used as a fuel in diesel engines. It burns well, but not as fast as kerosene. Many cars, most buses, trucks and ships have diesel engines.

Fuel oil is used as a fuel for heating in homes, offices and schools. It burns more slowly than kerosene or diesel so is no good as a fuel in engines.

Don't use it!

Engines, heaters and lamps are designed to burn just one sort of fuel. Another fuel would not work. So you cannot put fuel oil in an engine that is designed to run on petrol.

Oil for lubrication

The oil you put on your bicycle wheels or gears is called **lubricating** oil. It comes from crude oil. We use lubricating oil to make the parts of machines move more easily. It flows slowly and clings to the parts of machines. When two parts of a machine slide against each other a force called **friction** tries to stop them sliding. Putting lubricating oil between the surfaces helps them to glide past each other. It reduces friction.

Lubricating oils flow slowly and feel slimy.

On a bicycle, lubricating oil makes the wheels and gears move round smoothly.

We use lubricating oil on all sorts of moving parts, from door hinges to sewing machines, and even computers. The oil in an engine makes the parts move smoothly. If a car runs out of oil there is a lot of friction between the moving parts. Friction makes heat. As parts heat up they get slightly bigger and cannot move anymore. We also use grease on machines. Grease is oil that is made thick to stop it flowing away.

Chemicals from oil

We make many useful materials from chemicals that come from crude oil. They are called **petrochemicals**. The biggest use of petrochemicals is in making **plastics**.

These pellets are small chunks of plastic made from crude oil. They are ready to be made into plastic objects.

Fertilizers made from crude oil contain substances that plants need to grow.

A substance called ammonia comes from crude oil. Ammonia is the most important ingredient in **fertilizers**, which farmers use to make their crops grow better. Some household cleaners also contain ammonia.

Hundreds of other materials are made from petrochemicals too. Benzene is used to make a material called nylon. We make strong **fabrics** and small parts for machines from nylon. Toluene is used to make an explosive called TNT, which is used in tunnel building and mining.

Plastics from oil

The most important materials made from **petrochemicals** are **plastics**. The petrochemicals are the **raw materials** for making the plastics. Plastics have very different **properties** from the crude oil they are made from. Unlike oils, plastics are **solid** materials and are easy to make into complicated shapes. They last for a very long time because they do not **rot** away. Plastics can be hard and strong or soft and bendy. Many plastics are **waterproof** and **airtight**.

Emulsion paint contains millions of tiny bits of plastic that give the paint its colour.

This fabric has been woven
from plastic fibres.

The properties of plastic mean that it can be made into
an amazing number of different things. Carrier bags,
waterproof sheets, parts for machines and toys, boxes,
bottles and cases for machines are all made from plastic.
Plastic is also made into **fibres** that are woven into
plastic **fabrics**. It is also made into rubbery materials
for vehicle tyres, shoes and sink plugs.

Waxes and bitumen

After most of the **gases** and **liquids** have been taken out of crude oil a very thick liquid is left. This is made up of materials called petroleum waxes and **bitumen**.

A wax is a **solid** material that goes soft when it gets warm and **melts** when it gets hot. Most candles are made from petroleum wax. Melted wax at the top of a candle gets soaked up by the candle's wick and burns to make light. Wax is also **waterproof**. We use petroleum waxes to make things such as raincoats waterproof. Furniture polish contains wax that protects wood.

Petroleum waxes are also used in cosmetics such as face paints.

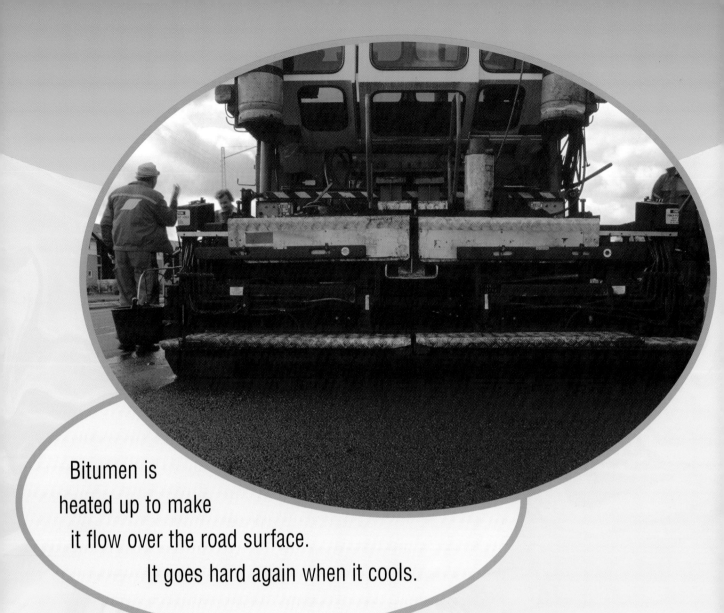

Bitumen is heated up to make it flow over the road surface. It goes hard again when it cools.

Bitumen on roads

When bitumen is cool it is so thick that it is like a solid. When it is warm it is runny and sticky. Most bitumen is used to make roads. It works like a glue that holds together the bits of stone in the road's surface. It also stops water getting into the road. Builders also use bitumen to make roofs waterproof.

Gases from oil

A **gas** is a substance that spreads out to fill the space it is in. You cannot see or feel most gases. Air is a gas. Crude oil contains gases such as butane and propane. We get them out by **refining** the oil. They burn very well and give out lots of heat without making dirty smoke. We use them as **fuels** for heating and cooking. Some cars and buses use gases for fuel instead of petrol or diesel.

This camping stove uses gas from the small containter. It is small and easy to carry.

Storing gases from oil

When we squeeze the gases from crude oil into a small space they turn into **liquids**. We store them in metal containers so they stay as liquids. As soon as we let them out they turn back to gas that we can burn.

The air in a hot-air balloon is heated by gas made from crude oil.

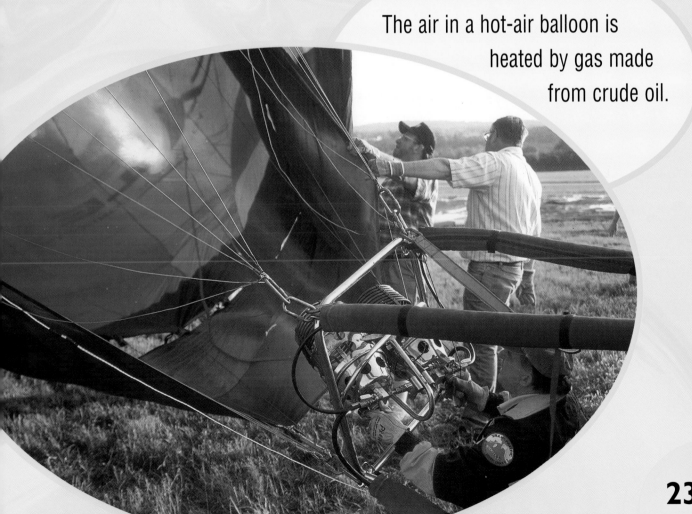

Natural gas

When **geologists** find crude oil they often find **gas** too. This gas is called **natural** gas. Natural gas is made from the remains of plants and animals that lived millions of years ago. So it is also a **fossil fuel** like crude oil.

Gas is moved along huge pipelines like this.

Natural gas is a very clean fuel. It burns without making smoke or any smell and is used in gas stoves.

Natural gas is a very good **fuel**. We can use it without **refining**. It makes lots of heat when it burns and does not make smoke. We burn gas for heating in open fires and in central heating boilers. We also burn it for cooking. Natural gas gets to our homes, schools and offices along underground pipes. Natural gas is also burned in power stations to help make **electricity**.

Biogas

*A gas like natural gas comes from **rotting** plants. We call it biogas. Sometimes you see biogas bubbling out of boggy ground. We can make biogas by rotting animal dung in special containers. Biogas is useful because it is a **renewable** fuel.*

Oil from plants

Oils are **liquids** that feel slimy and do not mix with water. Crude oil comes from the rocky ground beneath our feet. Rocks are made from **minerals**, so crude oil is called a mineral oil. We get oils from plants too. They are called vegetable oils.

Sunflower oil comes from the seeds of sunflowers. It can be used to make margarine.

Vegetable oil can be used to fry foods.

We use many vegetable oils for cooking and for making foods. For example, olive oil comes from the fruit of olive trees. We use olive oil for frying food and for making salad dressing. We use oil from sunflowers, peanuts, soya beans and coconuts for cooking too. Cooking oil moves heat from the cooking pan to the food.

We also use vegetable oils to make other materials. For example, the oil from the seeds of a plant called flax is called linseed oil. We use it to make paints and varnishes.

Oil and the environment

There is a limited store of crude oil under the ground. We are using oil much faster than new oil is being made. Eventually oil will run out, maybe in less than a hundred years time. We call oil a non-**renewable** material because once it is used we can never get it back. We can make oil last longer by using less of it every day. Plant oils are renewable because we can grow new plants.

Burning petrol and diesel makes gases such as carbon dioxide that come out of a car's exhaust.

Sea birds often suffer badly in oil spills.

Burning **fuels** from crude oil, such as petrol and diesel oil, releases **gases** into the air. One of these gases is called carbon dioxide. It is one of the gases that scientists believe is changing the world's weather. We must burn less fuel to stop these changes.

Oil spills

One of the ways we move crude oil to where it is needed is in huge ships called oil tankers. Sometimes these run aground and the oil spills out. The oil does not mix with water, it floats and spreads out. If it reaches the shore it can kill animals and plants that live there.

Find out for yourself

The best way to find out more about oil is to investigate for yourself. Ask an adult to show you oil that is used in your home, such as cooking oil and lubricating oil. Also look for products that are made from crude oil, such as plastics and rubber. Think about what makes each material good for doing that job. You will find the answers to many of your questions in this book. You can also look in other books and on the Internet.

Books to read

Science Answers: Grouping Materials, Carol Ballard (Heinemann Library, 2003)

Discovering Science: Matter, Rebecca Hunter (Raintree, 2003)

Energy Files: Oil and Gas, Steve Parker (Heinemann Library, 2003)

Using the Internet

Try searching the Internet to find out about things to do with oil. Websites can change, so if one of the links below no longer works, don't worry. Use a search engine, such as www.yahooligans.com or www.internet4kids.com. For example, you could try searching using the keywords 'oil exploration', 'butane' and 'oil spills'.

Websites

A great site, which explains all about different materials:
http://www.bbc.co.uk/schools/revisewise/science/materials/

A fun site that explains how oil is found and used:
http://www.petroleum.co.uk/education/ypg/ypg.htm

Glossary

airtight describes a material that does not let air pass through it

bitumen thick, sticky black material made from crude oil

electricity form of energy that flows along wires

fabric flat sheet of bendy material such as nylon

fertilizer material that contains nutrients that plants need to grow well

fibre long, thin, bendy piece of plastic

fossil fuel fuel made from the remains of animals and plants that died millions of years ago. Coal, oil and natural gas are fossil fuels.

friction force between two touching surfaces. It tries to stop the surfaces sliding past each other.

fuel material that burns well, making plenty of heat

fume smelly gas that comes from a liquid such as petrol

gas substance that spreads out to fill the space it is in

geologist scientist who studies rocks and fossils

liquid substance that takes the shape of whatever container it is put into

lubricate reduce friction by putting oil between two surfaces

melt turn from a solid to a liquid by heating

mineral material found in rocks

natural describes anything that is not made by people

petrochemical substance from oil or gas used to make other materials

piston part of an engine that is moved by steam or burning gas

plastic type of material made from chemicals found in crude oil and natural gas

property quality of a material that tells us what it is like. Hard, soft, bendy and strong are all properties.

raw material natural material that can be used to make other materials

renewable type of fuel or energy that is replaced naturally after we have used it

refine to split crude oil into its parts

rot to be broken down

solid substance that does not flow

waterproof describes a material that does not let water flow through it

Index